BIBLICAL ARCHAEOLOGY

A GENERATION OF DISCOVERY

SIEGFRIED H. HORN

Professor Emeritus, Andrews University

Biblical Archaeology Society
Washington, D.C.

Library of Congress Card Catalog Number 84-063096
ISBN: 0-9613089-1-5

This book is a revised and updated version of a monograph
published by Andrews University, Berrien Springs, Michigan,
under the title *Biblical Archaeology After 30 Years (1948-1978)*. The
monograph in turn was based on a lecture delivered at Andrews
University on October 22, 1978, on the occasion of the naming of
the Archaeological Museum for Siegfried H. Horn. This book is
now republished by special arrangement with Siegfried H. Horn
and Lawrence T. Geraty, Director, Institute of Archaeology, Andrews University.

Manufactured in the United States of America

CONTENTS

List of Illustrations

On the cover: A profusion of pillar figurines excavated at many sites in Israel. Dating to the Iron Age, ninth to seventh centuries B.C., the clay sculptures are probably fertility figurines.

INTRODUCTION

In the spring of 1948, a sensational discovery was made known to the world. The famous Dead Sea Scrolls had been found the year before in the wilderness of Judea near the Dead Sea. The year 1948 therefore serves as a convenient starting point for a survey of what has been achieved in the enormously exciting discipline of biblical archaeology.[1] It can truthfully be said that the discoveries made during these last 37 years easily dwarf those made during the preceding century in their total impact on a better understanding of the Bible.

The achievements of the last 37 years can be classified under seven headings: (1) The consolidation of ancient chronology; (2) the finding of texts bearing on the history of writing; (3) the discovery of ancient texts that have shed light on various periods of biblical history; (4) the discovery of ancient biblical manuscripts; (5) the sensational emergence of the Ebla texts of the pre-patriarchal age; (6) the excavation of key cities in the Holy Land, with some remarkable results; and (7) discoveries that have a particular bearing on the New Testament. I shall attempt in the following pages briefly to survey these discoveries and accomplishments and to evaluate their impact on biblical studies.

---

[1] I am well aware of the fact that many Palestinian archaeologists are unhappy that the archaeological work conducted in the Near East in general and in the Holy Land in particular carries the label "biblical archaeology." Yet no one will deny that many of the findings made in lands with which the Bible is concerned have a definite bearing on the Bible. Proof that students of the Bible, Jews as well as Christians, are interested in this work that sheds light on the Bible is the success of periodicals such as *Biblical Archaeology Review* (hereafter cited as *BAR*) and the *Biblical Archaeologist* (hereafter cited as *BA*) as well as the many books that carry similar names.

See on this subject and the controversy about the term "biblical archaeology" the following discussions in *BAR*: "Should the Term 'Biblical Archaeology' Be Abandoned?" VII:3 (May/June 1981): 54-57; "*BAR* Interviews Yigael Yadin," IX:1 (Jan./Feb. 1983): 16-23; "Annual Meetings Exhilarating; Debate over Biblical Archaeology Laid to Rest," X:2 (Mar./Apr. 1984): 10-11, 86-88; "A New Generation of Israeli Archaeologists Comes of Age," X:3 (May/June 1984): 60-61; "Jerusalem Rolls Out Red Carpet for Biblical Archaeology Congress," X:4 (July/Aug. 1984): 12-18; "The Relationship of Archaeology to the Bible," XI:1 (Jan./Feb. 1985): 6-8.

The appended footnotes with their citations of relevant publications will assist the reader in obtaining more detailed information.

Section of the Temple Scroll. "The Statutes of the King," contained in this portion of the Temple Scroll, the most recently discovered and the longest of the Dead Sea Scrolls, present the rights and duties of the king of Israel. This portion closely follows the text of Deuteronomy 17:14-16. (See discussion on p. 24.)

1

ANCIENT CHRONOLOGY

By 1948 a certain stabilization in the chronological scheme of the history of the ancient Near East had been reached. The discoveries of synchronisms at Ur and Mari, of Sumerian king lists, and of astronomical texts in Egypt and Mesopotamia had caused at least three revolutions in our understanding of ancient chronology, each of which resulted in the reduction of the dates for the earliest historical dynasties both in Egypt and in Mesopotamia.[2] The beginning dates of Egyptian history had by that time been reduced from the seventh millennium B.C. to about 3000 B.C., although it was not yet quite clear whether the starting date for the First Dynasty should be 3100, as many Egyptologists believed, or 300 years later, as others claimed. The same status of near consensus in dating the beginning of Mesopotamian history had been reached with differences between scholars that were of about the same range as in the area of Egyptian chronology. Also, the problems of the chronology of Old Testament history in the period of the Hebrew kings had finally been solved by the work of E. R. Thiele,[3] although his chronological scheme was not yet universally accepted in 1948.[4]

Since 1948 no startling discoveries have been made that have

---

[2] See the articles of William F. Albright: "Revolution in the Chronology of Ancient Western Asia," *Bulletin of the American Schools of Oriental Research* (hereafter cited as *BASOR*) 69 (Feb. 1938): 18-21; "The Chronology of Western Asia Before 1500 B.C.," *BASOR* 77 (Feb. 1940): 25-30; "A Third Revision of the Early Chronology of Western Asia," *BASOR* 88 (Dec. 1942): 28-36; cf. also my articles "A Revolution in the Early Chronology of Western Asia," *Ministry* 30:6 (June 1957): 4-8; "A Revolution in the Early Chronology of Egypt," *Ministry* 32:6 (June 1959): 29-33.

[3] "The Chronology of the Kings of Judah and Israel," *Journal of Near Eastern Studies* (hereafter cited as *JNES*) 3 (1944): 137-186. This work appeared later in an expanded form under the title *The Mysterious Numbers of the Hebrew Kings* (Chicago, 1951; rev. ed., Grand Rapids, Mich., 1965), and *A Chronology of the Hebrew Kings* (Grand Rapids, Mich., 1977).

[4] See for example Albright's "The Chronology of the Divided Monarchy of Israel," *BASOR* 100 (Dec. 1945): 16-22.

forced us to reduce or lengthen this chronological scheme. However, important discoveries made since then have consolidated these earlier conclusions. First, the Carbon 14 method of dating ancient organic material must be mentioned. After some years of experimentation, during which time the assumed half-life of Carbon 14 had to be changed, this method has reached a reasonable degree of accuracy for the historical periods of ancient times.[5] The results can be checked by datable material, such as inscribed wooden objects from Egypt, as well as by redwood trees and bristlecone pine trees, whose age can be determined by counting their tree rings.[6]

Although Carbon 14 dating has not significantly clarified the histories of such ancient civilizations as Egypt and Mesopotamia, for which we have abundant written records, its impact on our knowledge of cultures that left no historical written records is immeasurable. For example, during the last 35 years the origin of the great ruins of Zimbabwe (in the southern African country of Zimbabwe, formerly called Rhodesia) has been ascertained at between 1200 and 1450 A.D. by the Carbon 14 method; originally, guesses for these dates ranged from 1000 B.C. to 1000 A.D. The ages of the various ancient European and American cultures have also been dated—an accomplishment that a few decades ago no one thought would ever be possible.

Archaeological discoveries have filled gaps and reduced uncertainties in Mesopotamian chronology. The discovery of a new Assyrian king list (the SDAS Assyrian King List) by this writer in 1953, and the subsequent publication of both this list and the Khorsabad King List confirmed the Mesopotamian chronology of the second and first millennia B.C. as it had been established before 1948 and filled in gaps that still existed in chronological schemes.[7] The result of all this

---

[5] The professional literature on Carbon 14 dating is so immense that only a specialist can find his way through it. See the popular article, L. J. Briggs and K. Weaver, "How Old Is It?" *National Geographic* 114 (Aug. 1958): 234-255.

[6] See E. Schulman, "Bristlecone Pine, Oldest Known Living Thing," *National Geographic* 113 (Mar. 1958): 354-372; C. W. Ferguson, "Bristlecone Pine," *Science* 159 (1968): 839-846; C. Renfrew, "Ancient Europe Is Older Than We Thought," *National Geographic* 152 (Nov. 1977): 614-623.

[7] I. J. Gelb, "Two Assyrian King Lists," *JNES* 13 (1954): 209-230; Benno Landsberger, "Assyrische Königsliste und 'Dunkles Zeitalter,' " *Journal of Cuneiform Studies* 8 (1954): 32-45, 47-73, 106-133.

is that the uncertainties with regard to Mesopotamian dates amount to no more than 65 years for the second millennium B.C., and that the dates for the first millennium are practically certain.

The chronology of ancient Egypt has also been consolidated. In 1945, an important study published by Lynn H. Wood established an absolutely fixed date in the Egyptian chronology of the second millennium B.C.—the beginning of the 12th Dynasty in 1991.[8] In 1950, Richard Parker published an authoritative study on the Egyptian calendar systems and chronological problems; he settled many obscure points of Egyptian chronology and confirmed the date 1991 B.C. for the beginning of the 12th Dynasty of Egypt.[9] Since then the chronology of the kings of the 12th Dynasty has assumed an unassailable scheme.

Some other periods of Egyptian chronology are not so well established. It is now virtually certain that the First Dynasty began in the 31st century B.C. However, with the exception of the 12th and 26th Dynasties, all dates in ancient Egyptian history are still somewhat fluid. For some kings the uncertainty amounts to a few decades, for others to only a few years. On the whole, it can be said that the scheme of Egyptian chronology as arrived at in 1948 has stood the test of time.[10]

In 1953, Aramaic papyri found more than half a century earlier in Elephantine, Egypt, but hidden in a trunk in a New York warehouse until 1947, served in a most welcome way to solve chronological riddles. The papyri provided clear information for the first time about the Jewish calendar of the post-exilic period. The Elephantine papyri proved that those scholars were right who had insisted that the Jews dated the regnal years of Babylonian or Persian kings according to their own calendar, which began in the autumn, in contrast to the Babylonian-Persian calendar, which began in the spring.[11]

---

[8] "The Kahun Papyrus and the Date of the Twelfth Dynasty," *BASOR* 99 (Oct. 1945): 5-9.

[9] *The Calendars of Ancient Egypt* (Chicago, 1950), p. 69.

[10] For a convenient survey of the degree of reliability of Egyptian dates, see my review of E. Hornung's *Untersuchungen zur Chronologie und Geschichte des Neuen Reiches* (Wiesbaden, 1964) in *JNES* 25 (1966): 280-283.

[11] Emil G. Kraeling, *The Brooklyn Museum Aramaic Papyri* (New Haven, Conn., 1953);

Other discoveries, such as the Babylonian chronicle covering several years of Nebuchadnezzar's reign, settled questions of dates concerning the last years of the kings of Judah. This chronicle also provided a nearly exact day, month and year in biblical history—March 15/16, 597 B.C.—for the fall of Jerusalem at the time of King Jehoiachin.[12] No longer can it be said that the last years of the history of the kingdom of Judah are shrouded in mystery, as far as nonbiblical source material is concerned.

Generally then, the period since 1948 has been most satisfying for students interested in matters of ancient chronology. While many knowledgeable scholars, including W. F. Albright, were convinced by 1948 that stabilization had been reached,[13] their faith was fully vindicated as they saw one new discovery after another more or less confirm the results obtained in the field of ancient chronology. Practically all pertinent discoveries made since 1948 have either confirmed dates arrived at before 1948, or have modified them only slightly upward or downward. The result is that today most ancient dates of the historical periods are settled, and where uncertainties are still encountered, the margin of error is tolerable. Except for the beginning of Egyptian and Mesopotamian history, where a century of "give and take" must still be allowed, the range of uncertainty is no greater than a few years, or in many cases no greater than one year or two years. This gratifying accomplishment has made it possible to reconstruct ancient history so that it approaches a degree of accuracy that it never had before.[14]

Siegfried Horn and Lynn H. Wood, *The Chronology of Ezra 7* (Washington, 1953; rev. ed. 1970); id., "The Fifth-Century Jewish Calendar at Elephantine," *JNES* 13 (1954): 1-20. For a dissenting voice on the conclusions reached in the works by Horn and Wood, see Richard Parker, "Some Considerations on the Nature of the Fifth-Century Jewish Calendar at Elephantine," *JNES* 14 (1955): 271-274.

[12] D. J. Wiseman, *Chronicles of Chaldaean Kings* (London, 1956), p. 33.

[13] Albright, "Bible After Twenty Years of Archaeology," *Religion in Life 21 (1952)*: 538.

[14] See the recently published chronological tables in *The Cambridge Ancient History*, 3rd ed. (Cambridge, 1970-1975), vol. 1, part 2, pp. 994-1003; vol. 2, part 1, pp. 819-823; vol. 2, part 2, pp. 1038-1045.

2
HISTORY OF WRITING

The history of writing was well-known in 1948. The 19th century saw the successful deciphering of the Egyptian hieroglyphs. The cuneiform script of the Sumerians that was adopted by other nations such as the Assyrians, Babylonians, and Hittites was also deciphered. During the first half of the 20th century two hitherto unknown alphabetic scripts that were invented in the middle of the second millennium B.C. were deciphered: first the proto-Sinaitic hieroglyphic script by Alan Gardiner in 1915;[15] and second the Ugaritic cuneiform script by Hans Bauer and Edouard Dhorme, in 1930.[16] These achievements proved those scholars wrong who had maintained that no alphabetic systems of writing had existed before the first millennium B.C., since both systems had been in use during the second millennium B.C.

During the last three-and-a-half decades the work of deciphering unknown scripts has continued. The Hittite hieroglyphic system of writing was deciphered with the help of the bilingual Phoenician-Hittite inscriptions discovered at Karatepe in southern Turkey in 1947.[17] The Minoan Linear B script was read in 1952 by the brilliant young architect Michael Ventris, who died four years later in a car accident.[18] However, these triumphs in the field of writing have only

---

[15] "Egyptian Origin of the Semitic Alphabet," *Journal of Egyptian Archaeology* 3 (1916): 1-16. Many scholars have since worked on the proto-Sinaitic inscriptions, of which some have been discovered in Sinai, others in Palestine. After having dealt with this subject many times in articles, Albright published his latest views in *The Proto-Sinaitic Inscriptions and Their Decipherment* (Cambridge, Mass., 1966).

[16] See Maurice Pope, *The Story of Archaeological Decipherment* (New York, 1975), pp. 117-122.

[17] Ibid., pp. 136-145. This relates the history of the decipherment of Hittite hieroglyphs, including the progress made before the discovery of the Karatepe inscriptions.

[18] Ibid., pp. 159-179; see also John Chadwick, *The Decipherment of Linear B* (New York, 1958).

7

marginal importance for biblical studies, although they opened new vistas in our understanding of the ancient world.

Of much greater importance to our field is the progress made in west-Semitic paleography, the science of dating ancient documents written in Aramaic, Phoenician, Hebrew, and related languages, on the basis of the form of the script used. While Greek paleography had become a reliable discipline, dating Greek manuscripts within an error margin of only a few years, the dating of undated Hebrew manuscripts was still more or less learned guesswork. The first pioneering work in west-Semitic paleography was done in 1937 by W. F. Albright. Albright gathered the few dated Hebrew and Aramaic inscriptions and worked out a rudimentary paleography of these scripts,[19] which proved substantially sound as more dated material became available in subsequent years.

It was this work that in 1948 helped date the Hebrew scrolls found near the Dead Sea. Many scholars, among them some eminent Semitists, were skeptical and suggested that the Dead Sea Scrolls, dated by Albright and his students to the pre-Christian era, came from a much later age or were even forgeries. However, as more scroll material from the various caves of the wilderness of Judea— some of it discovered by archaeologists—and later also from Masada, became available, this situation changed radically. Some of the scroll material found later bore dates, which put the science of Hebrew paleography on a sound basis. Foremost among those who have worked in the field are Joseph Naveh, [20] Frank Moore Cross[21] and S. A. Birnbaum,[22] but a host of other scholars have also made contributions. The result is that the discipline of Hebrew-Aramaic paleography has become a science so well established that any document, be it

---

[19] "A Biblical Fragment from the Maccabean Age: The Nash Papyrus," *Journal of Biblical Literature* (hereafter cited as *JBL*) 56 (1937): 145-176.

[20] *Early History of the Alphabet* (Jerusalem, 1982).

[21] Of his many paleographic studies see especially his "The Development of The Jewish Scripts," in G. E. Wright, ed., *The Bible and the Ancient Near East: Essays in Honor of William Foxwell Albright* (Garden City, N. Y., 1961), pp. 133-202. The notes on pp. 188-202 provide an almost exhaustive bibliography.

[22] "The Qumrân (Dead Sea) Scrolls and Paleography," *BASOR*, Supplementary Studies, nos. 13-14 (1952), pp. 1-52; id., *The Hebrew Scripts*, 2 vols. (London, 1954-57; Leiden, 1971)

Manual of Discipline. Badly damaged and still partially rolled up, this Dead Sea Scroll still displays clearly the work of the Essene scribe who copied the text in the first century B.C. The scroll sets out the detailed code of rules of the Essenes, an ascetic, highly structured and fiercely religious Jewish sect that lived in a commune at Qumrân, on the edge of the Dead Sea.

an inscription or a manuscript, can without any hesitation be assigned a date within a 50-year range.

Some interesting discoveries have also shed unexpected light on the antiquity of the sequence of the alphabetic characters. The sequence of the Hebrew alphabet letters, as is well-known, went back to the beginning of the first millennium B.C. This fact is attested by the acrostic psalms in the Bible, some of which were composed in the tenth century B.C.; and also by the Greek alphabet, which had been taken over from the Phoenicians certainly not later than around 800 B.C. Since the sequence of the letters of both the Phoenician and Greek alphabets is the same, it could be concluded that the origin of the ABCs went back at least to the beginning of the first millennium B.C.

However, no one thought that the origin of the sequence of the alphabet went back to the 16th and 15th centuries B.C., when the various alphabetic writing systems seem to have been invented. This was first revealed by a discovery made in 1949 at Ras Shamra, ancient Ugarit, and by another discovery made at 'Izbet Ṣarṭah, possibly ancient Eben-ezer, in 1976.

During the 1949 excavations at Ras Shamra, a 14th-century B.C. tablet came to light containing all alphabetic cuneiform characters of Ugaritic in sequence. This sequence turned out to be the same as the one still used today, 3,500 years later, in Hebrew-Aramaic dictionaries.[23]

An ostracon discovered at 'Izbet Ṣarṭah in 1976 and dated to about 1200 B.C., the period of the Judges, contains the Hebrew alphabet in the sequence known to 20th-century students of Hebrew. The only deviations are a missing *mem*, probably the result of a scribal error, and the transposition of the letters '*ayin* and *pe*. The '*ayin-pe* transposition in this abecedary agrees with the sequence of the Hebrew alphabet found in three acrostic compositions of the Book of Lamentations, which traditionally have been attributed to

---

[23] Albright, "Some Important Recent Discoveries: Alphabetic Origins and the Idrimi Statue," *BASOR* 118 (Apr. 1950): 12-14; Cyrus H. Gordon, "The Ugaritic 'ABC' " *Orientalia* 19 (1950): 374-376; E. A. Speiser, "A Note on Alphabetic Origins," *BASOR* 121 (Feb. 1951): 17-21. Later several more such "abecedaries" were found at Ras Shamra, for which see Charles Virolleaud, *Le palais royal d'Ugarit, II* (Paris, 1957), pp. iv-vi, 199-203.

Jeremiah. It seems that the Hebrew alphabet was memorized in two different ways by the ancients: according to one tradition with the

'Izbet Ṣarṭah abecedary. This proto-Canaanite inscription, the oldest Hebrew alphabet ever discovered, appears on a sherd only 3½ inches wide and 6 inches long. It was found in the storage pit of an Israelite house at 'Izbet Ṣarṭah that dated to about 1200 B.C.

sequence *pe-'ayin,* and according to another tradition with the sequence *'ayin-pe.*[24]

The result of these discoveries and studies is that the origin and the development of alphabetic writing is now well-known. There can no longer be any doubt that fully developed alphabetic writing systems existed in the time of Moses, making it possible for him and his successors to write books in a script that all could learn. It is equally well established that these simple systems of writing, in contrast to the cumbersome and intricate hieroglyphic and cuneiform scripts of Egypt and Mesopotamia, quickly spread throughout Palestine and Syria and thus made it possible for religious works such as those preserved in the Bible to become "peoples' books."

---

[24] Moshe Kochavi, "An Ostracon of the Period of the Judges from 'Izbet Ṣarṭah," *Tel Aviv* 4 (1977): 1-13; Aaron Demsky, "A Proto-Canaanite Abecedary Dating from the Period of the Judges and Its Implications for the History of the Alphabet," ibid., pp. 14-27, contains a good bibliography on the history of the alphabet on pp. 25-27; "BAR Readers to Restore Israelite Village from the Days of the Judges," *BAR* V:1 (Jan./Feb. 1979: 34; David Epstein, "Reader Inspects Restoration of Israelite Village," *BAR* V:6 (Nov./Dec. 1979): 58.

3

DISCOVERIES OF TEXTS

A phenomenal increase in textual material, written in alphabetic scripts and composed in several west-Semitic languages, has occurred in recent years. For example, in 1948 we possessed about 90 Hebrew inscriptions, not counting seals and seal impressions. These inscriptions consisted of the Siloam Tunnel inscription, two inscriptions from Silwan, not yet deciphered at that time, the Gezer calendar on a stone plaque, and 86 ostraca, of which 63 had been found at Samaria and 21 at Lachish. The Lachish ostraca are still considered one of the most sensational inscriptional finds made in Palestine during the period between the two world wars.[25] Since that time the pace of discovery of inscriptional material in Hebrew and Aramaic has greatly accelerated.

Aside from the Dead Sea Scrolls, which are discussed separately, Hebrew inscriptional materials, principally ostraca, have been discovered at many sites. Arad, for example, produced more than 100 Hebrew and Aramaic ostraca, some of extraordinary importance. On one of them reference is made to a Temple of Yahweh, although it is not clear whether the Temple in Jerusalem or the local Yahweh temple is meant.[26]

At Kuntillet 'Ajrud, a site about 30 miles south of Kadesh-Barnea in northern Sinai, some Phoenician inscriptions and numerous

---

[25] All Hebrew inscriptional material up to 1934 was published by David Diringer, *Le iscrizioni antico-ebraiche palestinesi* (Florence, 1934), supplemented in 1951 by Sabatino Moscati, *L'epigrafia ebraica antica* (Rome, 1951).

[26] The full collection of the Arad ostraca was first published in Hebrew by Yohanan Aharoni in 1975, but has been available in English under the title *Arad Inscriptions* since 1981 (Jerusalem, 1981). However, many of the important ostraca were published and discussed in the following English articles by Aharoni: "Letter from a Hebrew King?" *BAR* VI:1 (Jan./Feb. 1980): 52-56; "Hebrew Ostraca from Tel Arad," *Israel Exploration Journal* (hereafter cited as *IEJ*) 14 (1964): 1-7; "Arad: Its Inscriptions and Temple," *BA* 31 (1968): 2-32; "Three Ostraca from Arad," *BASOR* 197 (Feb. 1970): 16-42.

Hebrew inscriptions of the ninth or eighth century B.C. were discovered in 1975-1976. The inscriptions were in ink on various vessels and on plaster or incised on vessels of clay and stone. The preliminary reports of this interesting inscriptional material show that Yahweh, Israel's God, appears repeatedly in connection with Asherah, in expressions such as "May you be blessed by Yahweh and

Lachish ostracon. More than 20 ostraca like this one, the only collection of Hebrew letters from the time of the First Temple, were found in a guardroom in Lachish's city wall. They were written by a Judean officer at the height of Babylonia's war on Israel in the early sixth century B.C. The ostracon shown here is Letter No. 3. Written in an iron-base ink, it contains the warning of a prophet and refers to another letter received from a royal official named Tobiah. This ostracon is the earliest nonbiblical document to use the Hebrew word for a prophet, navi.

Holy of Holies in temple at Arad. The earliest Israelite place
of worship yet excavated, this temple dates to the tenth to
seventh centuries B.C. Three steps lead to the sacred niche,
which is flanked by replicas of two incense altars; the original
altars are now in the Israel Museum in Jerusalem.
Excavators found one small standing pillar, or massebah, in
the niche. Two earlier stelae were built into one wall and
covered with plaster. Near this temple, 100 ostraca inscribed
in Hebrew and Aramaic were discovered.

by his Asherah,"[27] From the biblical records, we know that by the
time of King Abijam of Judah, Solomon's grandson, an Asherah had
been set up and worshipped in Jerusalem. This image was later
removed by Abijam's pious son and successor Asa (1 Kings 15:13).
Under King Manasseh, an Asherah even stood in the Temple of
Jerusalem (2 Kings 21:3, 7). The Asherah cult became especially
strong in the northern kingdom of Israel under King Ahab, when it
was introduced by Ahab's Phoenician wife, Jezebel, who also installed prophets to serve this deity (1 Kings 16:33; 18:19). Scholars

[27] Suzanne Singer, "Cache of Hebrew and Phoenician Inscriptions Found in the Desert," *BAR*
II:1 (Mar. 1976): 33-34; Ze'ev Meshel and Carol Meyers, "The Name of God in the
Wilderness of Zin," *BA* 39 (1976): 6-10; 40 (1977): color plates A and B facing p. 66; Meshel,
"Kuntilat 'Ajrud," *IEJ* 27 (1977): 52-53; id., "Did Yahweh Have a Consort?" *BAR* V:2 (Mar./
Apr. 1979): 24-34.

disagree about what the Asherah of Yahweh at Kuntillet 'Ajrud was. André Lemaire interprets it as a sacred tree;[28] William Dever recently interpreted the Asherah in the Kuntillet 'Ajrud inscription as a consort of Yahweh.[29] The Bible makes clear that Yahweh's prophets, Elijah and others, fought vigorously against this trend of polytheism and idol worship. The Kuntillet 'Ajrud texts are therefore extremely interesting witnesses to the prominence given the Canaanite Asherah at certain periods in the religious history of ancient Israel.

Kuntillet 'Ajrud inscription. This reproduction shows an enigmatic scene that was painted on a storage jar at Kuntillet 'Ajrud, a site that may have been a travelers' rest stop in the southern Negev. Some archaeologists identify the figure far left as Yahweh and the one in the center as the Egyptian demigod Bes; others say that both standing figures are Bes. The seated lyre player is the subject of heated debate. Some say her name is Asherah and identify her as the consort of Yahweh. Others say she is simply a musician.

---

[28] "Who or What Was Yahweh's Asherah?" *BAR* X:6 (Nov./Dec. 1984): 42-51. See also Meshel, "Did Yahweh Have a Consort?" *BAR* V:2 (Mar./Apr. 1979): 24-34.

[29] William G. Dever, "Asherah, Consort of Yahweh? New Evidence from Kuntillet 'Ajrud," *BASOR* 255 (Summer 1984): 21-37; id., "Iron Age Epigraphic Material from the Area of Khirbet el Kôm" *Hebrew Union College Annual* 40/41 (1969-1970): 139-204.

In 1960 at Meṣad Ḥashavyahu, 10½ miles southwest of Tel Aviv, a 14-line letter came to light; it was written in the seventh century B.C. by a poor laborer and addressed to the governor or military commander of the district.[30] The letter petitions for the return of the laborer's garment, which had been impounded by one Hoshaiah, evidently the foreman of a royal harvesting corvée. The petitioner complains that he was accused of having unlawfully ceased labor before the Sabbath started. He insists that he had completed his work, and that he had witnesses to that effect. This case brings to mind the biblical injunction not to keep overnight a poor man's garment given as a pledge, since he may need it to protect himself from the cold (Exodus 22:27). Albright's introduction to his translation of the letter contains references to a few of the many articles that have appeared since the first publication of this interesting ancient Hebrew letter.

During the excavations at Masada, leather manuscripts of biblical and non-biblical books were found, as well as the ostraca used as lots by the defenders to determine who would carry out the gruesome duty of killing their compatriots before the Romans could capture the fortress.[31]

At Deir 'Alla in the Jordan Valley, large fragments of inscriptions written in ink on plaster came to light during the excavations at that site in the spring of 1967. Written about 700 B.C., they contain visions and curses of the prophet Balaam, the son of Beor, as well as the reactions of the addressees. These plaster inscriptions, written in a hitherto unknown dialect of Aramaic,[32] seem to have originally

---

[30] Joseph Naveh, "A Hebrew Letter from the Seventh Century B.C.," *IEJ* 10 (1960): 129-139; Albright in J. B. Pritchard, ed., *Ancient Near Eastern Texts*, 2nd ed. (1969), p. 568.

[31] Yigael Yadin, "The Excavation of Masada—1963/64, Preliminary Report," *IEJ* 15 (1965): 103-114; id., *Masada* (New York, 1966), pp. 187-191, 201.

[32] Jacob Hoftijzer, "The Prophet Balaam in a 6th-Century Aramaic Inscription," *BA* 39 (1976): 11-17. In the final publication of the inscriptions Hoftijzer's co-author, G. van der Kooij, raised the date to about 700 B.C.; see Hoftijzer and van der Kooij, *Aramaic Texts from Deir 'Alla* (Leiden, 1976), p. 96. The following review articles of the work of Hoftijzer and van der Kooij make significant contributions to the understanding of these very difficult and fragmentary texts: A. Caquot and André Lemaire, *Syria* 54 (1977): 189-208; P. Kyle McCarter, *BASOR* 239 (Summer 1980): 49-60; B. A. Levine, *Journal of the American Oriental Society* 101 (1981): 195-205; Jo Ann Hackett, *The Balaam Text from Deir 'Alla* (Chico, Cal., 1984).

*Mesad Hashavyahu letter. In this seventh-century B.C.
Hebrew inscription, a farmer complains to the governor that
an officer had confiscated his garment unjustly. The cursive
script indicates that the letter was probably penned by a
professional scribe who recorded the dictated words of the
farmer. The ostracon was found near the fortress gate at
Mesad Hashavyahu, a small, coastal fortress of the First
Temple period.*

covered either a stone stele or a wall at a prominent public place. The
texts are of the utmost interest to the student of the Bible; they are
the first pre-exilic witnesses to a somewhat obscure prophet who
played a role in the early but vague history of the nation of Israel
when it was struggling to gain a foothold in the promised land
(Numbers 22-24). It is interesting to note that the Balaam texts were
found at Deir 'Alla in the lower Jordan Valley, not far from the site
where Balaam's oracles concerning Israel were pronounced according to the biblical tradition (Numbers 22:1).

    In 1961 a cave was found at a site called Khirbet Beit Lei, some five

King Herod's palace-fortress at Masada. The first-
century B.C. three-tiered palace at the northern end of
Masada's rocky prow is clearly evident in the center of
this photo. Immediately to the right of the palace but not seen
in the photo are remains of the siege ramp that allowed the
Romans to breach the Zealot defenses on the mountaintop.
Excavator Yigael Yadin discovered not only elaborate baths
and storage buildings but also exquisite frescoes and a cache
of fragments of biblical manuscripts.

miles east of Lachish. The cave had been used as a burial cave in the time of the Hebrew kings. Joseph Naveh dates the cave to about 701 B.C., when Lachish was conquered and destroyed by the Assyrians under King Sennacherib; however Frank Cross dates it more than 100 years later, when Lachish was conquered by Nebuchadnezzar of Babylon. Several crude representations of boats and human figures, as well as inscriptions in the old Hebrew script scratched into the soft limestone walls were found in this Iron Age burial cave. The inscriptions, now on display in the Israel Museum in Jerusalem, are extremely difficult to read. Naveh, the first scholar to edit the texts, translates them as follows:

"Yahweh (is) the God of the whole earth;
the mountains of Judah belong to him, to
the God of Jerusalem.
The (mount of) Moriah thou hast favored,
the dwelling of Yah, Yahweh.
[Ya]hweh deliver (us)!"[33]

The Cross translation, made after much additional study, is:

"I am Yahweh thy God: I will accept
the cities of Judah, and will redeem Jerusalem.
Absolve (us) o merciful God!
Absolve (us) o Yahweh!
Deliver (us) o Yahweh!"[34]

Whatever the correct translation, it is evident that the inscription expresses a pious citizen of Judah's trust in his God in the face of tremendous odds, possibly when he was mourning friends or relatives killed in the conquest of Lachish. While expressing his trust in the God who redeemed Jerusalem when other cities fell, he was also pleading for mercy and deliverance.

Although I have limited my survey of discoveries made during the last 37 years mainly to Palestine and Syria, discoveries have been made in other areas as well. Let me once more point to the cache of Aramaic papyri from Elephantine, which turned up in New York in

---

[33] Naveh, "Old Hebrew Inscriptions in a Burial Cave,"*IEJ* 13 (1963): 74-92.

[34] Frank Moore Cross, "The Cave Inscriptions from Khirbet Beit Lei," in J. A. Sanders, ed., *Near Eastern Archaeology in the Twentieth Century: Essays in Honor of Nelson Glueck* (Garden City, N.Y., 1970), pp. 299-306.

1947. These papyri, published in 1953 by Emil Kraeling, not only revealed to us the nature of the Jewish calendar of the post-exilic period, as was mentioned on p. 5, but also shed much welcome light on the cultural, legal and social conditions of the Jewish colonists there who had migrated to Egypt before the exile.[35]

In 1948, André Dupont-Sommer published the fragment of an Aramaic letter found at Saqqara, Egypt, in 1942. It was written by Adon, king of a Philistine city (probably Ekron), to an Egyptian king. The letter, written during one of the Babylonian invasions led by Nebuchadnezzar, contains a plea for immediate military help to rescue King Adon and his land. This interesting document has produced a large number of linguistic and historical studies.[36]

Other Aramaic documents which have greatly helped us in the study of Aramaic, a language represented in some books of the Old Testament, are the letters of Arsames, the Persian satrap of Egypt. These were found in 1926 in the original leather pouch in which they had been transported, and were published in 1954 by G. R. Driver.[37] And last but not least, eight papyri found at Hermopolis in 1945 deserve mention. These papyri, published in 1966 by E. Bresciani and M. Kamil, refer to the worship of the Queen of Heaven, a goddess worshipped also by the apostate Jews whom Jeremiah encountered when he came to Egypt (Jeremiah 44:19).[38]

Our understanding of the Ammonite language has been greatly increased during the period under review. We have had a fair knowledge of the Moabite language since the 1868 discovery of the Moabite stone with its 34-line Moabite inscription; but, for a long time Ammonite was practically unknown. In 1969, when I published the Amman Citadel Inscription,[39] the whole corpus of Ammonite inscriptions consisted of 12 seals, most of them bearing only one name, and one stone inscription 12 characters in length. Ammonite inscriptions now number more than 40, thanks to the discovery of

---

[35] See n. 11.

[36] Bezalel Porten, "The Identity of King Adon," *BA* 44 (1981): 36-52. This article contains a comprehensive bibliography on the subject.

[37] *Aramaic Documents of the Fifth Century* B.C. (Oxford, 1954).

[38] "Le Lettere aramaiche di Hermopoli," *Atti della Accademia Nazionale dei Lincei;* Classi di scienze morali storiche e filologiche, serie 8, Memorie vol. 12, fasc. 5 (1966), pp. 357-428.

[39] Horn, "The Amman Citadel Inscription," *BASOR* 193 (Feb. 1969): 2-13.

new inscriptions, including the Amman Citadel Inscription with eight incomplete lines, and the Bronze Bottle Inscription from Tell Siran containing eight complete lines.[40] The Heshbon Expedition, sponsored by Andrews University, also contributed to the number of Ammonite documents with its discovery of several ostraca, one of which has 11 lines.[41] All of this material has rescued the Ammonite language from obscurity and shows us the place this language occupied in the genealogical tree of west-Semitic languages.

Before I leave the subject of texts, I should not fail to mention the many hundreds of seals and of inscribed seal impressions on clay bullae that have been found in recent years. Most Hebrew names mentioned on these seals and seal impressions find parallels in biblical names, although we can never be certain that the seals belonged to the actual biblical characters who bore those names. Exceptions are probably the seals of "Manasseh the son of the king"[42] and "Jehoahaz the son of the king."[43] These presumably belonged to Manasseh, the son of Hezekiah, and to Jehoahaz, the son of King Josiah, when these owners of the seals were still crown princes. In addition, several recently published inscribed seal impressions almost certainly were created by seals that had belonged to biblical figures. These include impressions of seals belonging to: "Baruch, son of Neriah, the scribe," who was the secretary of the prophet Jeremiah (Jeremiah 36:4, 32; 45:1); "Jerahmeel, son of the king," sent by King Jehoiakim to arrest both Baruch and Jeremiah (Jeremiah 36:26); "Gemariah, son of Shapan," a royal courtier (Jeremiah 36:10-12, 25); and "Baalis," king of the Ammonites (Jeremiah 40:14). Furthermore, the actual seal of Baruch's brother "Seraiah, son of Neriah" (Jeremiah 51:59) has also recently come to light.[44]

[40] Henry O. Thompson and Fawzi Zayadine, "The Tell Siran Inscription," *BASOR* 212 (Dec. 1973): 5-11.

[41] Cross, "Ammonite Ostraca from Heshbon," *Andrews University Seminary Studies* 13 (1975): 1-20.

[42] Nahman Avigad, "A Seal of 'Manasseh Son of the King,' " *IEJ* 13 (1963): 133-136.

[43] Avigad, "A Group of Hebrew Seals," *Eretz Israel* 9 (1969): 134.

[44] Avigad, "Jerahmeel and Baruch," *BA* 42 (1979): 114-118; Yigal Shiloh, "Jerusalem, City of David," *IEJ* 33 (1983): 131; the seal impression of Baalis, discovered at Tell el-'Umeiri in Jordan in 1984, is still unpublished.

4

DEAD SEA SCROLLS

The finding of the scrolls in the wilderness area of eastern Judea has revolutionized and increased our understanding of Judaism during the intertestamental period. As a result of the Dead Sea Scroll discoveries, the discipline of textual criticism of the Hebrew Old Testament, which hardly existed before 1948, is on a firm foundation. I will not dwell on the history of the discoveries, which is well-known,[45] but will briefly summarize the text material that has come into the hands of scholars from the caves and valleys of eastern Judea.

(1) The first scrolls were discovered in a Qumrân cave in 1947. News of this discovery reached the world a year later, the year I have chosen as the beginning date for this survey. In the succeeding years, up to 1956, scroll fragments were found in ten more caves near Qumrân. A complete scroll, the now famous copy of Isaiah, was found in Cave 1. Some scrolls from Caves 1 and 11 were nearly complete; others came into the hands of scholars as large or small fragments, which in some cases could be pieced together. The assembled pieces provided major portions of literary works or other documents. The sheer amount of fragmentary material is formidable. Cave 4, for example, produced 35,000 scroll fragments, coming from more than 400 manuscripts.

With the exception of some material from Cave 4, of which much still remains unpublished, the texts from the Qumrân caves are

---

[45] The story of the discoveries of the Dead Sea Scrolls has been told in many books. The following accounts were written by men directly involved in the discovery and acquisition of the scrolls: Millar Burrows, *The Dead Sea Scrolls* (New York, 1955), pp. 3-69; id., *More Light on the Dead Sea Scrolls* (New York, 1958), pp. 3-36; Yigael Yadin, *The Message of the Scrolls* (New York, 1957), pp. 15-52; Athanasius Yeshue Samuel, *Treasure of Qumrân; My Story of the Dead Sea Scrolls* (Philadelphia, 1966); John C. Trever, *The Untold Story of Qumrân* (Westwood, N. J., 1965).

available in published form.[46] These scrolls, which were all produced prior to the end of the first Jewish-Roman war (66-73 A.D.), contain samples of all Hebrew Old Testament books except the book of Esther. They also contain a large number of Jewish non-canonical writings, some apocryphal and pseudepigraphal works already known when the scrolls were discovered, but mostly literary works that had not been known before.[47]

The largest of all the scrolls—27 feet long—and possibly the most important one, was called "The Temple Scroll" by its editor, Yigael Yadin. Probably found in Cave 11, it was for many years in the hands of an Arab antiquities dealer. In the closing hours of the 1967 Six-Day War, Yadin tracked down the scroll for the Israeli government. Yadin believed that the scroll's contents show that it was for all practical purposes the Torah of the Essenes. It contains instructions for the building of the Temple, statutes of the king's duties, laws for the community, and regulations for the annual feasts, offerings and gifts.[48]

(2) In 1951, the caves of Wadi Murabba'at, east of Bethlehem, produced scroll material from the second century A.D., among which was a large portion of a scroll of the Minor Prophets and documents pertaining to the Bar Kokhba revolt against the Romans. This material was published in 1961.[49]

(3) A cave discovered in 1961 in the Naḥal Ḥever, southwest of Ein

---

[46] The scroll material from Cave 1 has been published by Burrows, Trever and William H. Brownlee, *The Dead Sea Scrolls of St. Mark's Monastery,* 2 vols. (New Haven, Conn., 1950, 1951); E. L. Sukenik, *The Dead Sea Scrolls of the Hebrew University* (Jerusalem, 1955); D. Barthélemy and J. T. Milik, *Discoveries in the Judean Desert, I: Qumrân Cave I* (Oxford, 1955); Avigad and Yadin, *A Genesis Apocryphon* (Jerusalem, 1956).

The scroll material from Caves 2 and 3 and 5-10 was published by M. Baillet, Milik, and Roland de Vaux, *Discoveries in the Judaean Desert of Jordan, III: Les 'Petites Grottes' de Qumrân* (Oxford, 1962).

Of the scroll material from Cave 4, the following three volumes have so far appeared: John M. Allegro and A. A. Anderson, *Discoveries in the Judaean Desert of Jordan, V: Qumrân Cave 4: I (4Q158-4Q186)* (Oxford, 1968); de Vaux, Milik et al., *Discoveries in the Judaean Desert, VI: Qumrân Grotte 4,* vol. 2 (pt. 1, *Archéologie;* pt. 2, *Tefillin, Mezuzot et Targums)* (Oxford, 1977); Baillet, *Discoveries in the Judaean Desert, VII: Qumrân Grotte 4,* vol. 3 *(4Q482-4Q520)* (Oxford, 1982).

Of the scrolls from Cave 11 the following two works have appeared: J. A. Sanders, *Discoveries in the Judaean Desert of Jordan, IV: the Psalms Scroll of Qumrân Cave 11* (Oxford, 1965); J. P. M. van der Ploeg and A.S. van der Woude, *Le Targum de Job de la grotte XI de Qumrân* (Leiden, 1971); D. N. Freedman and K. A. Mathews, *The Paleo-Hebrew Leviticus Scroll (11QpaleoLev)* (Winona Lake, Ind., 1985).

Gedi, also contained a large number of documents from the second century A.D. The documents were left by Jews who had fled into the desert during the Bar Kokhba revolt. Besides many secular documents in Hebrew, there were some papyri written in the Nabataean script and fragments of biblical books. Only samples of this material have been published so far.[50]

(4) Text material of biblical and non-biblical books was also found during the excavations of Masada in 1963 and 1964. This material, antedating the fall of the fortress in 73 A.D., has been published only in preliminary form.[51]

(5) In the inaccessible Wadi Dâliyeh, northwest of Jericho, some Samaritan scrolls of the fourth century B.C. were discovered in 1962. These are secular documents that allow us to reconstruct the succession of the governors of Samaria from the time of Nehemiah to Alexander the Great. The documents themselves have not yet been published, but summaries of their contents are available. [52]

What are the results of all these phenomenal text discoveries made during the last 37 years in the wilderness of Judea?

(1) The scrolls have provided samples of books of the Hebrew Bible from the period of Jewish history when the Bible text was still fluid—before the Council of Jamnia toward the end of the first century A.D.; but they also contain samples of biblical books copied after Jamnia. Our knowledge of the process of collecting, editing and copying sacred writings, and the process of canonization of the

[47] See Cross, *The Ancient Library of Qumrân and Modern Biblical Studies* (Garden City, N. Y., 1976), pp. 120-180.

[48] Yadin, *The Temple Scroll*, 3 vols. (Jerusalem, Hebrew edition 1977; English edition 1984); "The Temple Scroll—The Longest and Most Recently Discovered Dead Sea Scroll," *BAR* X:5 (Sept./Oct. 1984): 32-49.

[49] Pierre Benoit, Milik, de Vaux, *Discoveries in the Judean Desert, II: Les grottes de Murabba'ât* (Oxford, 1961).

[50] Yadin, "The Expedition to the Judean Desert, 1960; Expedition D," *IEJ* 11 (1961): 40-52; id., "The Expedition to the Judaean Desert, 1961; Expedition D—The Cave of the Letters," *IEJ* 12 (1962): 227-257.

[51] See note 31.

[52] Cross, "The Discovery of the Samaria Papyri," *BA* 26 (1963): 110-121; id., "Papyri of the Fourth Century B.C. from Dâliyeh," in Freedman and J. C. Greenfield, eds., *New Directions in Biblical Archaeology* (Garden City, N. Y., 1969), pp. 63-79; id., "The Historical Importance of the Samaria Papyri," *BAR* IV:1 (Mar. 1978): 25-27; Paul W. Lapp, "Bedouin Find Papyri Three Centuries Older than Dead Sea Scrolls," *BAR* IV:1 (Mar. 1978): 16-24.

Qumrân caves. In these caves that pock the desolate landscape of Qumrân near the Dead Sea, members of the Essene sect hid hundreds of scrolls to protect them from conquering Romans in the first century A.D. First discovered in 1947, the scrolls have immeasurably increased our understanding of Judaism from the second century B.C. to the first century A.D.

Hebrew Bible, is far from complete. However, some of these Hebrew texts from the Dead Sea area—which are more than a thousand years older than the earliest texts we had in 1948—have immeasurably increased our understanding of what happened to the Hebrew text before the Masoretic age in the tenth through eighth centuries B.C., from which time we can trace our present Hebrew Bible. They have shown that the Hebrew text had undergone much less change than was thought possible before these early copies became available.[53] The result is that the Hebrew Bible text is treated with greater respect by scholars today than it has been for a long time.

On the other hand, the scroll evidence does not support the claims of those fundamentalists who believe in *verbal* inspiration and in a slavish, unalterable transmission of the text, for it shows clearly that different recensions of biblical books were in circulation before Jamnia and that scribes of the pre-Jamnia era had felt at liberty to modernize the text when they copied it. This applies not only to changes in spelling and the choice of modern synonyms for out-moded words and antiquated grammatical forms and expressions, but also in some cases to alterations in the text that seemed to the scribes to need clarification.

(2) The scrolls, in conjunction with the results of the excavations at Khirbet Qumrân, have resurrected the Jewish sect of the Essenes. The little information we had about the Essenes in 1948 was based on statements made by Josephus, Philo, Pliny the Elder, and Dio of Prusa. But the Essene sect is never mentioned in the Bible, and all its literature had been thought to have vanished until it emerged from the Qumrân caves.[54]

(3) While the biblical scholar is mainly interested in the biblical scrolls, it should not be overlooked that the caves of Qumrân have given us a wealth of Jewish literature, most of which was hitherto unknown. Although much of this literature comes from one Jewish sect, the Essenes, it demonstrates that an immensely rich Jewish

---

[53] See the papers of Patrick W. Skehan, Sanders and Freedman, in Freedman and Greenfield, eds., *New Directions*, pp. 89-138.

[54] Cross, *The Ancient Library of Qumrân*, pp. 146-189; Jerome Murphy-O'Connor, "The Essenes and Their History," *Revue Biblique* 81 (1974): 215-244; id., "The Essenes in Palestine," *BA* 40 (1977): 100-124.

Temple Scroll. This portion of the famed Temple Scroll contains commands for cleansing after contact with a leper and commands for purifying the house of a dead person. According to Yigael Yadin, who published the scroll in 1977, the Temple Scroll is the Essenes' Torah, or book of laws, written between 134 and 104 B.C. Nearly half the scroll is taken up with the Essenes' elaborate plans for the building of the Temple.

literature, religious, historical and literary in nature—for the most part lost now—must have existed in the time of Jesus and the apostles.

(4) The caves of the Judean wilderness have provided original documents about the Bar Kokhba revolt and the ensuing second war of the Jews against the Romans. No history of the second Jewish-Roman war has survived, whereas much is known of the first Jewish-Roman war from the extensive writings of the historian Josephus.

The discovery of the Dead Sea Scrolls has spawned a completely new discipline of biblical studies, has caused the production of thousands of articles and hundreds of books, of which the bibliography alone fills several volumes,[55] and has resulted in the founding of a learned journal, the *Revue de Qumrân*, entirely devoted to this discipline. Neither theologians nor biblical scholars can afford to ignore the rich store of information that the study of the scrolls has provided in an unending stream during the last several decades.

---

[55] Christoph Burchard, *Bibliographie zu den Handschriften vom Toten Meer*, 2 vols. (Berlin, 1957, 1965), covering the publications from 1948 to 1962; W. S. LaSor, *Bibliography of the Dead Sea Scrolls 1948-1957* (Pasadena, Cal., 1958); B. Jongeling, *A Classified Bibliography of the Finds in the Desert of Judah, 1958-1969* (Leiden, 1971); Joseph A. Fitzmyer, *The Dead Sea Scrolls: Major Publications and Tools for Study* (Missoula, Mont., 1975). The *Revue de Qumrân* has presented bibliographies in every issue since it began publication in 1958.

5
EBLA AND THE AGE
OF THE PATRIARCHS

The discoveries made during the years between the two world wars brought evidence to light concerning the world and times of the patriarchs, evidence that seemed to prove the essential historicity of the patriarchal stories. Commenting about the abundant material, William F. Albright said in 1950: "There is scarcely a single biblical historian who has not been impressed by the rapid accumulation of data supporting the substantial historicity of patriarchal tradition."[56]

However, in recent years new onslaughts on the historicity of the patriarchal stories have been made that resemble in some respects the heyday of Wellhausenism.[57]

Julius Wellhausen (1844-1918) was a German theologian who, building on the theories of previous critical biblical scholars, in several widely read books eloquently promoted a hypothesis of the development of the early books of the Bible, such as the five books of Moses. According to this hypothesis, stories of folklore and historical events were transmitted—some orally and others in written form—for many ages. However, during the post-exilic period these various sources, classified according to hypothetical original authors as J (Yahwist), E (Elohist), P (Priestly) and D (Deuteronomist), were assembled and skillfully combined by an unknown editor to whom the symbol R (Redactor) was given. To make these collective works generally acceptable their authorship was attributed to famous men of antiquity such as Moses, Joshua or Samuel. The result of this reasoning was that the stories of Israel's pre-history and early history,

---

[56] *The Biblical Period* (Pittsburgh, 1950), p. 3.

[57] Thomas L. Thompson, *The Historicity of the Patriarchal Narratives* (Berlin, 1974); John Van Seters, *Abraham in History and Tradition* (New Haven, Conn., 1975).

Ebla tablets, as the excavators found them. Nearly 20,000 inscribed tablets were strewn around the excavated archive room of the royal palace of Ebla. In the right of this picture are tablets lying in parallel layers; these probably fell from the shelves above, where they had been filed upright like books..

Hailed as the most sensational find in biblical archaeology since the Dead Sea Scrolls, the Ebla tablets today challenge scholars to decipher their language in order to reveal their message.

such as the periods of the patriarchs, the Exodus and the occupation of the promised land, were considered as nothing but reflections of old traditions of a somewhat unreliable historicity. The following quotation from one of Wellhausen's works may serve as an example of his views: "From the patriarchal narratives it is impossible to obtain any historical information with regard to the patriarchs; we can only learn something about the time in which the stories about them were first told by the Israelite people. This later period, with all its essential and superficial characteristics, was unintentionally projected back into hoary antiquity, and is reflected there like a transfigured mirage." (*Prolegomena zur Geschichte Israels*, 6th ed. [Berlin, 1905], p. 316.)

Then, just when biblical scholars, reacting to these new attacks on the historicity of the patriarchal stories, had re-examined the foundations of their positions and sharpened their weapons for a defense of the patriarchs, help seemed to come from an entirely unexpected side—Ebla. Who among biblical historians had ever heard of this name before 1976, when the first reports appeared about some sensational discoveries made in an ancient city of Syria? And, now, less than ten years later, Ebla has become a household word and is just as well-known among biblical scholars and ministers as Qumrân or Ras Shamra-Ugarit.

It is still too early to evaluate the findings made at Tell Mardikh, ancient Ebla, where reportedly 20,000 cuneiform tablets came to light during the four seasons of excavations—from 1974 to 1977. This discovery has been labeled variously as the most sensational find ever made in the field of biblical archaeology or the greatest discovery since the finding of the Dead Sea Scrolls. However, the first fantastic claims about the tablets and their contents made after the initial news about their discovery became known have not all been confirmed by further study.[58] Part of the reason for this lies in the complexity of the cuneiform texts, and in the original, understandable rush to publish.

Most people do not realize how difficult it is to read and understand mid-third millennium B.C. cuneiform texts, and they have no idea of the complexities of the writing systems of that time. The Ebla texts reveal that the scribes of Ebla used Sumerian cuneiform script and the Sumerian language in most documents, but they also experimented in writing their own Semitic language, called Eblaite, using the same Sumerian script. This script was imperfectly suited to

---

[58] For example Giovanni Pettinato first announced that the names of the five cities of the plain of Genesis 14, among them Sodom and Gomorrah, are mentioned in the Ebla texts. Further studies have cast doubts on some of the earlier readings of the names in question as well as on the identification of the cities si-da-mu and è-ma-ra of the Ebla texts with Sodom and Gomorrah. See on this controversy the following: Pettinato's claim that the five cities are found in the Ebla tablets was made in his article, "Gli archivi reali de Tell-Mardikh-Ebla; riflessionie prospectivi," *Rivista Biblica Italiana* 25 (1977): 236; Shanks, "*BAR* Interviews Giovanni Pettinato," *BAR* VI:5 (Sept./Oct. 1980): 46-52. On Pettinato's change of reading of two of the names, see Mitchell Dahood, *BA* 41 (1978): 143. Questions on the readings of Pettinato were expressed in the following articles: Paolo Matthiae, "Ebla," *BA* 43 (1980): 133-134; Robert Biggs, "The Ebla Tablets," ibid., 82. Alfonso Archi, "Further Concerning Ebla and the Bible," *BA* 44 (1981): 151-152.

this purpose since it consisted in great part of word signs or logograms, rather than syllabic characters that reveal how words were spelled and pronounced. Where the Eblaite scribe uses Sumerian word signs, a modern Sumerologist knows their meaning, but not how they were pronounced in Eblaite. In the same way, an American who has never learned French understands the numeral 20 when he sees it in French, but does not know that in French it is not pronounced "twenty," but "vingt."[59]

Immediately after the discovery of the thousands of tablets at Ebla, only one epigrapher trained in Sumerology, Professor Giovanni Pettinato of the University of Rome, was available to study their contents. Scholars and interested laypeople, in the meantime, were understandably curious and impatient to learn more about this large, 4½-millennia-old archive of documents. In response to demands to reveal what the texts contained, some provisional announcements were made, based upon only a cursory reading of some of the texts. It is therefore understandable that the first translations, in many cases made within a year after the discovery of the tablets, had to be revised after more thorough study by Pettinato himself and especially after several other Sumerologists had worked with them. In the ten years or so that have passed since the Ebla tablets were found, a team of several Sumerologists has formed an International Committee for the Study of Ebla Texts, and many texts have been published in books and articles. Therefore, a more mature evaluation of the material is now possible. Two semi-popular works written by the excavator and the first epigrapher provide a fairly good idea of what the Ebla texts reveal.[60]

The results of ten years of Ebla research show that Eblaite, as the new language is called, is more closely related to biblical Hebrew than

---

[59] See the explanations of Biggs in the article "The Ebla Tablets," *BA* 43 (1980): 76-87. Biggs is well qualified to appreciate the problems connected with the Ebla texts since he published the tablets from Abu Salabikh, Iraq, which are similar to the Ebla texts, come from about the same time and pose about the same problems of reading and understanding as the Ebla tablets.

[60] Matthiae, *Ebla—An Empire Rediscovered* (Garden City, N. Y., 1981); Pettinato, *The Archives of Ebla—An Empire Inscribed in Clay.* With an Afterword by Dahood (Garden City, N. Y., 1981). See also the earlier work of C. Bermant and M. Weitzman, *Ebla—An Archaeological Enigma* (London, 1979) which gives a very good summary of the material as far as it was available some five years ago.

Ugaritic is; and that among the tablets are bilingual (Sumerian and Eblaite) word lists and some literary texts, although the majority are concerned with economic matters. We learn that some kings of Ebla ruled over an empire that reached from the Mediterranean Sea to the Persian Gulf; that their capital had a population of 260,000; and that their civil service consisted of 11,000 employees. The archives reveal that the kings of Ebla had trade relations with much of the known world of their day, from Egypt in the south, to Mesopotamia in the north and east, and that the names of many Palestinian cities occur among the 5,000 names of cities so far found on the tablets. Among them are such well-known biblical cities as Hazor, Lachish, Megiddo, Gaza, Dor, Joppa, Ashdod, Akko, Ashtarot, and Salem. The latter is the name of Jerusalem during the patriarchal period (Genesis 14:18). One of the six kings of Ebla carried the name Ebrum, in which we recognize the biblical name Eber, borne by one of Abraham's ancestors (Genesis 10:21), although these were not the same individuals. Many personal names that appear in the documents have a good biblical sound: Michael, Abram, Israel, Ishmael, Micaiah, Esau, Saul and David.

The dates of the origin of the Ebla tablets are still somewhat uncertain. The archaeologist Matthiae dates the tablets, on the basis of archaeological and stratigraphical evidence, between 2400 and 2250 B.C.; Pettinato, the Ebla epigrapher, on the other hand, dates the archive more than a century earlier, between 2580 and 2450 B.C. The discovery of a seal impression of the Egyptian king Pepi I at Ebla in 1979, supported Matthiae's dating of the archive more than Pettinato's.[61]

These remarks on Ebla are made in a tone of cautious optimism and even enthusiasm; yet they also contain many questions. The reason for this lack of certainty is that the discoveries are still too recent and consequently have not yet been carefully examined and digested.

---

[61] Paul C. Maloney, "Assessing Ebla," *BAR* IV:1 (Mar. 1978): 7; Matthiae, *Ebla—An Empire Rediscovered*, pp. 9-10.

6

EXCAVATIONS
OF BIBLICAL SITES

The number of biblical cities excavated east and west of the river Jordan is enormous. In addition to numerous minor archaeological explorations, about 80 major archaeological expeditions have worked in the Holy Land since World War II. I must limit my survey to a few sites and refer you for information on the others to the four-volume work *Encyclopedia of Archaeological Excavations in the Holy Land*.[62]

(1) *Jericho*. When our survey started we still believed that John Garstang, during his excavations in the 1930s, had found the walls of Jericho as they had fallen in Joshua's time. This interpretation was contradicted by Kathleen Kenyon's excavations at Jericho between 1952 and 1958. Kenyon found that the walls destroyed by an earthquake and interpreted by Garstang as the walls of the Late Bronze Age had actually fallen down many centuries before Joshua's time, in the Early Bronze Age. To everyone's surprise, Kenyon found almost nothing from the Late Bronze Age city, the city destroyed by the Israelites, and concluded that the forces of nature and humanity had obliterated nearly all vestiges of that city. However, her work showed that Jericho was the oldest inhabited and fortified city ever excavated. The strong round tower of neolithic times, which she discovered, was built before pottery had been invented. It is a mighty witness for the existence of an inventive genius and a cooperative achievement in that early period of this world's history.

Excavations conducted intermittently by other expeditions since

---

[62] Edited by Michael Avi-Yonah and Ephraim Stern, this work (hereafter referred to as *EAEHL*) is published by the Israel Exploration Society in Jerusalem. Volumes I-IV were issued from 1975 to 1978. The individual articles have been written by expert archaeologists, in most cases by the excavators of the sites themselves, and are accompanied by good bibliographies and pictures.

Frigidarium *at Herodian Jericho. A graceful lattice pattern of stones nearly encircles the "cold room" substructure of the baths at Herod's Jericho palace. This pattern of uniformly cut small stones laid in diagonal rows was a style of Roman wall-building used from the first century B.C. to the second century A.D. The second-century B.C Hasmonean kings of Israel and Herod the Great, in the first century B.C., built complexes of palaces, pools and gardens in Jericho as luxurious retreats from Jerusalem's winter cold.*

1950 at the ruins of New Testament Jericho have uncovered the remains of Hasmonean structures, as well as of the extensive and luxuriously built palace structures of Herod the Great, who died in this palace.[63]

(2) *Bab edh-Dhra*. This site, located on the Lisan peninsula in the Dead Sea, was discovered in 1924, but excavations were not carried out until 1965, when Paul Lapp began the first of his three excavation seasons there. In 1975, Walter Rast and Thomas Schaub resumed the excavations. The ancient town at Bab edh-Dhra flourished in the Early Bronze Age, when it and the surrounding area were densely inhabited. Lapp estimated that the cemetery, one of the largest ancient cemeteries ever discovered in Palestine, contained some 20,000 tombs, in which about 500,000 people were buried together with some three million pottery vessels and other objects.

The recent explorations of the area south and southeast of Bab edh-Dhra have brought to light the remains of four additional ancient cities located in a straight line south of Bab edh-Dhra: Numeira, 13 km (c. 8 mi.) to the south, Safi, 13 km (c. 8 mi.) further south, Feifa, 10 km (c. 6 mi.) south of Safi, and Khanazir, 6 km (c. 4 mi.) to the south of Feifa. All of these cities existed in the Early Bronze Age, and it seems that they were all destroyed sometime before 2000 B.C. Some scholars have cautiously suggested connecting these five cities with the "Cities of the Plain" of Genesis 18 and 19. If this suggestion should prove correct, then the patriarchal period, which has usually been identified with the Middle Bronze I Age, would have to be raised into the late phases of the Early Bronze Age, in the last centuries of the third millennium B.C. It is too early, however, at this point of the explorations of Bab edh-Dhra and the sites south of it to come to any firm conclusions.[64]

---

[63] Kathleen M. Kenyon, *Digging Up Jericho* (New York, 1957); Kenyon, G. Foerster and Gabriela Bacchi, "Jericho," *Encyclopedia of Archaeological Excavations in the Holy Land* 2: 550-575; E. Netzer, "The Winter Palaces of the Judean Kings at Jericho at the End of the Second Temple Period," *BASOR* 228 (1977): 1-13.

[64] Amnon Ben-Tor, "Bab edh-Dhra," *EAEHL* 1: 149-151; Walter E. Rast and R. Thomas Schaub, "Survey of the Southeastern Plain of the Dead Sea, 1973," *Annual of the Department of Antiquities of Jordan* 19 (1974): 5-53; id., "Preliminary Report of the 1979 Expedition to the Dead Sea Plain, Jordan," *BASOR* 240 (1980): 21-61; id., "Have Sodom and Gomorrah Been Found?" *BAR* VI:5 (Sept./Oct. 1980): 26-30; id., "The Southeastern Dead Sea Plain Expedition," *Annual of the American Schools of Oriental Research* 46 (1981).

(3) *Shechem.* After Jerusalem, Shechem was one of the most important cities in Palestine. With some interruptions, this city played a great role in the history of Israel from the patriarchal period down to the time of the Maccabees. Excavations were carried out at Shechem, first by Austrian-German expeditions in 1913 and 1914, and again from 1926 to 1934, under several directors, and then by an American expedition from 1956 to 1972, in which I participated for several seasons. The results of this work have immeasurably increased our knowledge of the city's ancient history. Excavation of the sacred area revealed a courtyard sanctuary and a later fortress temple dedicated to El-berith "the god of the covenant." This temple, which was destroyed by Abimelech, the son of the judge Gideon (Judges 9), has provided us with a date in the Judges period, for which dates from non-biblical sources are usually difficult to obtain. The fortifications and domestic areas of the various periods of Shechem's checkered history have been uncovered; so have the foundations of the Samaritan temple on one of the summits of Mt. Gerizim, as well as those of a Canaanite temple on the northeastern slope of Mt. Gerizim.[65]

Most recently a structure identified as an Israelite altar has been excavated on the northeastern slope of Mt. Ebal. Dating to the 13th to 12th centuries B.C., considered to be the time of Joshua, the altar suggests the possibility that it may be the altar built by Joshua and described in Deuteronomy 27, 28.[66]

(4) *Hazor.* This large Canaanite and Israelite city in upper Galilee was excavated under Yigael Yadin's direction from 1955 to 1958 and from 1968 to 1970. Hazor consisted of a fortified lower city of 70 hectares (173 acres) occupied from the 18th to the 13th centuries B.C., and a citadel of 12 hectares (30 acres) that was occupied from the 27th century B.C. until the Hellenistic period. The city experienced several destructions. Yadin interpreted the 13th-century-B.C. destruction as having been the work of the Israelites under Joshua. However, it is possible that this destruction should be attributed to

---

[65] G. Ernest Wright, *Shechem, the Biography of a Biblical City* (New York, 1965); Robert J. Bull, "The Excavations of Tell er-Ras on Mt. Gerizim," *BA* 31 (1968): 58-72.

[66] Adam Zertal, "Has Joshua's Altar Been Found on Mt. Ebal?" *BAR* XI:1 (Jan./Feb. 1985): 26-42.

the Israelites' war under Deborah and Barak against Hazor (Judges 4-5), while an earlier destruction, assigned by Yadin to either Thutmos III or Amenhotep II, may have been carried out by Joshua.

During the last seasons of excavation, an underground water system, constructed in the ninth century B.C., was uncovered. It consists of a cylindrical shaft about 16 m (c. 52 ft.) in diameter and 30 m (c. 98 ft.) deep. At the bottom of the shaft is a sloping tunnel, some 4.75 m (c. 15 ft.) high and 35 m (c. 115 ft.) long, which ends at a pool situated at the natural water level. The whole installation testifies to the importance of Hazor in the time of the Hebrew kings.

Besides Canaanite temples and other structures of unusual inter-

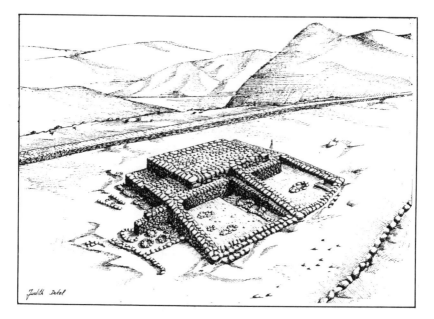

Artist's reconstruction of Mt. Ebal altar. This nine-foot-high structure stands alone near the summit of Mt. Ebal. It dates to Iron Age I (1220-1000 B.C.), the time archaeologists assign to the settlement of the Israelites in Canaan. The excavator, Adam Zertal, suggests that this altar may have been built by Joshua, as described in the Bible in Joshua 8:30. "Then Joshua built an altar unto the Lord God of Israel in Mount Ebal."

est, a Solomonic city gate was excavated at Hazor. The gate was identical to city gates found at Megiddo and Gezer. Since these three cities, in addition to Jerusalem, are listed in 1 Kings 9:15 as the principal objects of Solomon's building activities, it is not strange to find in them identical public structures probably built by the same architect and according to the same plans.[67]

(5) *Dan.* Dan started out as a Canaanite fortress. In the biblical records, the Egyptian execration texts, and the cuneiform tablets of Mari, it was known as Laish. In the 12th century B.C., the city was conquered by the Israelite tribe of Dan, and at that time its name was changed. Since Dan was the northernmost city and fortress of Israel, the limits of the country were frequently referred to in the Bible as reaching "from Dan to Beersheba" (1 Samuel 3:20 and elsewhere). Dan gained notoriety when King Jeroboam I built one of two national shrines of the northern kingdom there—and installed a golden calf as a cult object; the other shrine was built in Bethel.

Excavations at Tel Dan, known until the foundation of the State of Israel as Tell el-Qadi, were begun in 1966, under the direction of Avraham Biran, and have continued to the present time. The identification of the site was confirmed with the discovery in 1976 of a stone inscribed to "the god who is in Dan."

The excavations at Dan brought to light for the first time the remains of the large pre-Israelite city of Laish, which covered about 50 acres and may have had a population from 7,500 to 10,000. The most interesting discoveries from that period concern the city's fortification system, which consisted of sloping ramparts of earth that overlaid a stone core. A well-preserved triple-arched gateway of brick built in the 18th century B.C. was an unexpected discovery. It is the earliest arched gateway known so far. A tomb attributed to pre-Israelite Laish, dated by its contents to the 14th and 13th centuries B.C., was also discovered. It contained local ware as well as a rich selection of imported Mycenean painted pottery vessels, two vessels of Cypriote origin, bronze and ivory objects, and gold and silver jewelry.

---

[67] Yadin, "Hazor," *EAEHL*, 2: 474-495. On the Solomonic gates of Gezer and Megiddo, see William G. Dever, "Gezer," ibid., pp. 436-437, 441; and Yadin, "Megiddo," ibid., 3: 851, 854; id., *Hazor—The Rediscovery of a Great Citadel of the Bible* (London, 1975).

Middle Bronze Age gateway at Tel Dan. This arched mudbrick gateway, part of an 18th-century B.C. fortification system, was found fully preserved in 1979 by archaeologist Avraham Biran. For unknown reasons, the Canaanites had buried the gate after using it for only 30 to 40 years, thus insuring its preservation for nearly 4,000 years.

Tel Dan inscription. These three lines in Greek and one in Aramaic refer to a person who made a vow to the "god who is in Dan," or alternately, to the "god of the Danites." The tablet confirms the identity of the site as Dan, also called Laish in the Bible.

Cultic installation or an olive press? When this installation was discovered by Tel Dan excavator Avraham Biran, he identified it as a cultic installation. Now, some archaeologists believe that the installation is in fact a tenth- or ninth-century B.C. olive press, one of the earliest ever found in Israel.

*Throne within the Israelite gate at Tel Dan. Either a
king or a cult statue probably sat on this stone platform
uncovered at Tel Dan. Three round, socketed bases, two
to the left of the platform, one to the right, suggest that
posts were inserted in the holes to support a canopy over
the throne.*

During the Israelite period, the city had an elaborate gateway
consisting of an inner and outer gate and a stone-paved square. An
unusual structure excavated in that square either supported a king's
throne or a cult statue. On top of the mound, a large stone platform
approached by a monumental stairway was uncovered. In its first
phase, the platform measured 23 ft. by 59 ft., but in its later stage it
measured 59 ft. by 62 ft. This was probably the *bamah*, or "High
Place," on which Jeroboam's golden calf was worshipped.[68]

(6) *Arad.* Arad lies in the Negev, the southeastern desert of Judea.
Here, for the first time, the remains of a Hebrew temple were

---

[68] Avraham Biran, "Tel Dan," *EAEHL*, 1: 313-320; id., "Tel Dan," *BA* 37 (1974): 26-51; id.,
"Tel Dan Five Years Later," *BA*, 43 (1980): 168-182; id., "The Triple-Arched Gate of Laish at
Tel Dan," *IEJ* 34 (1984): 1-19; John C. H. Laughlin, "The Remarkable Discoveries at Tel
Dan," *BAR* VII:5 (Sept./Oct. 1981): 20-30.

Charioteer vase from Tel Dan. Found in a magnificent tomb, this 14th-century B.C. Mycenean krater is an unusually large and fine example of the Aegean potters' craft. The black and red figured vessel testifies to thriving trade across the ancient Mediterranean.

uncovered. Excavations at Arad conducted by Yohanon Aharoni from 1962 to 1967 uncovered a temple that may have originally been built in the time of Solomon, when that king tolerated the construction of shrines to other gods. It continued in use—rebuilt once in the ninth century B.C.—probably until the time of King Josiah, when such cult places were destroyed. The temple of Arad escaped destruction because, in the new town planning carried out in the seventh century B.C., part of the city wall was run right over the temple, thus covering it and all its cult paraphernalia. In this way the temple was preserved for the archaeologist who uncovered it more than 2,500 years later. So at Arad we have a sample of the type of schismatic temples that existed in pre-exilic Judah, temples that several prophets denounced. More than a hundred ostraca also were found at Arad, one of them referring to the "Temple of Yahweh," as already mentioned in the discussion of texts (see p. 13).[69]

(7) *Beersheba.* Tell Beersheba, excavated by Aharoni from 1969 until his untimely death in 1976, is not the Beersheba of the patriarchs. That earlier site should probably be sought underneath the modern city of Beersheba. The excavated ancient city, which lies a short distance to the east of modern Beersheba, existed only during the period of the Israelite kings. The most important discovery made at this site was a large stone altar, 1.6 m (63 in.) high, with horns at its four corners. Although small horned altars, probably used in private homes, have been found in several Palestinian excavations such as those at Megiddo and Shechem, this is the first time that a large horned altar that must have served the public in a regular sanctuary during the period of the Hebrew kings has come to light. Its discovery confirmed the interpretation of Amos 5:5 and 8:14 as referring to a schismatic sanctuary at Beersheba in the time of the prophet Amos.[70]

(8) *Ramat Raḥel.* This is a small site, halfway between Jerusalem and Bethlehem, where Aharoni conducted excavations from 1959 to 1962. The excavator has plausibly argued that Ramat Raḥel should be identified with biblical Beth-Haccherem. At this site the remains of a nearly totally destroyed royal palace of the last kings of Judah were found. No objects were discovered in the ruins of that palace, indicating that it had probably been thoroughly looted by the Babylonian forces when they destroyed it, either in 597 B.C. when they took King Jehoiachin into exile, or during the siege of Jerusalem, 588-586 B.C. However, several proto-Aeolic stone capitals that had once crowned columns and a stone balustrade from a window were found there. The latter architectural feature is known from representations found on ivory plaques that depict a woman looking through a window whose lower part consists of a balustrade like the one discovered at Ramat Raḥel. The Ramat Raḥel balustrade is made up of a row of small columns, decorated with a drooping petal motif

---

[69] Aharoni, "Arad," *EAEHL*, 1: 74-75, 82-89.

[70] Aharoni, "Beersheba," ibid., pp. 160-168; id., "The Horned Altar of Beer-sheba," *BA* 37 (1974): 2-6; Ze'ev Herzog, "Beer-Sheba and the Patriarchs," *BAR* VI:6 (Nov./Dec. 1980): 12-28.

*Beersheba horned altar. The disassembled stones of this
restored Israelite "horned" altar for animal sacrifice were
found built into a late eighth-century B. C. wall in
biblical Beersheba, to the east of modern Beersheba.
"Horns," or stylized, raised points mark the corners of
the top row of stones. The altar was probably dismantled
at the time of Hezekiah's religious reforms, about 715 B.C.*

and topped by small capitals of the proto-Aeolic type, joined together
at the edges of the volutes. Furthermore, a potsherd found during
the excavations contains a drawing that shows a bearded king with
curled hair, who is dressed in an ornamented robe with short sleeves
and is sitting on a high decorated chair. Since the sherd is local ware,
the drawing must be that of a local artist, and since it was found in a
royal palace, it is tempting to see in this picture the representation of
one of the last kings of Judah.[71]

(9) *Qumrân.* Khirbet Qumrân had been known as an ancient ruin
site for a long time, but no one had attached any great historical

---

[71] Aharoni, "Beth-Haccherem," in D. Winton Thomas, ed., *Archaeology and Old Testament
Study* (Oxford, 1967), pp. 171-184.

significance to the site. However, when Hebrew manuscripts were discovered nearby in one cave after another, this ruin was investigated in order to learn whether a connection existed between the people who had occupied Qumrân and the people who had left the scrolls in the caves. In 1951, Roland de Vaux conducted soundings, and when the excavators brought to light pottery that was identical with the pottery that had been discovered in the first cave, large-scale excavations of the ruins were conducted, from 1953 to 1956. These excavations revealed that Khirbet Qumrân had been a monastery-like community center of the Essenes. Here the members of the sect worked, ate and worshipped together in a communal life, although they spent the nights in scattered caves located in the vicinity. The compound contained several open-air pools, fed by an aqueduct that brought water from the mountains west of Qumrân. Some of the pools served as reservoirs for drinking water, while others were needed for the ritual washings of the members of the sect; these ritual baths contained stairways for access into the water. Furthermore, the excavations brought to light a pottery shop where the members of the sect made their own vessels, a kitchen full of cutlery, a dining hall, an assembly room where they worshipped, and long benches and tables which had been used in a scriptorium. The benches and tables consisted of wooden frames, now disintegrated, which had been covered on all sides by layers of plaster. Also some ink wells were found with the tables and benches.

At Ain Feshkha, an oasis two miles south of Qumrân, the Essenes operated a farm that provided them with their necessities of life. Here the farm buildings were excavated. A study of the Essene literature found in the caves, combined with the results of the excavations at Qumrân, has allowed us to reconstruct the history, life style, and religious beliefs and customs of the Essene sect.[72]

(10) *Jerusalem.* Some of the most important excavations ever carried out in the Holy City have been conducted in the last decades, first by Kathleen Kenyon from 1961 to 1967,[73] and after the Six-Day War by Israeli scholars.[74] These excavations have settled some of the most

---

[72] de Vaux, *Archaeology and the Dead Sea Scrolls* (London, 1973).

[73] Kenyon, *Digging Up Jerusalem.*

[74] Yadin, ed., *Jerusalem Revealed* (Jerusalem, 1975).

nettling problems of the history of the ancient city. Among those unsettled questions were the following: (1) Was the Gihon Spring accessible from inside the city of the Jebusites and of David? (2) Was the western hill included in Old Testament Jerusalem and, if so, since when? (3) Was the site of the Church of the Holy Sepulchre inside or outside the city in Christ's time?

On the eastern slopes of the hill of Ophel and just to the west of and above the Gihon Spring, Kenyon excavated part of the Jebusite wall of the Jerusalem that David conquered. In this way, she solved a vexing problem that had worried archaeologists ever since a stretch of city wall excavated by R. A. F. Macalister and J. G. Duncan in the 1920s had been interpreted as part of the Jebusite wall with some repair work visible that was attributed to King David. This Macalister-Duncan wall lay to the west of the entrance of the sloping ramp that led to "Warren's Shaft" and a rock-cut tunnel to the Gihon Spring. Hence the entrance to the water system leading to the spring lay outside the protective city wall. Kenyon found that the Macalister-Duncan wall with its tower and rampart was built in Nehemiah's time and later. The true Jebusite wall, of which she found clear vestiges, lay further down the slope of the hill to the east of the entrance to the underground water works, which thus lay well within the city wall.[75]

Since 1978, excavations have been carried out in the "City of David," the southeastern hill of ancient Jerusalem, under the direction of Yigal Shiloh. A tremendous bastion of pre-Davidic Jerusalem and parts of the city wall of the period of the monarchy have been excavated, and the ancient water system around the Gihon Spring has been thoroughly explored. These excavations reveal much about the topography of the city of Jerusalem before King Solomon's time. They also present the architectural history of the area when it formed only the southeastern part of a widely expanded capital of the kingdom.[76]

---

[75] Kenyon, *Digging Up Jerusalem*, pp. 76-97; see especially figures 16 and 17.

[76] Only preliminary reports on these excavations have appeared so far: Shiloh, "Jerusalem, the City of David," *IEJ* 28 (1978): 274-276; 29 (1979): 244-246; 30 (1980): 220-221; 32 (1982): 157-158; 33 (1983): 129-131; 34 (1984): 57-58; id., "The Rediscovery of Warren's Shaft," *BAR* VII:4 (July/Aug. 1981): 24-39.

Gihon Spring. The water bubbling from the ground into this chamber was essential to life in ancient Jerusalem. Several systems of tunnels and shafts were constructed at different times to provide protected access to the water in times of siege.

*Warren's Shaft. In this photo from the early 20th century, we see
the vertical shaft that bears the name of its discoverer,
Captain Charles Warren. The shaft, possibly enlarged from
a natural geologic fissure, was part of a tunnel complex
probably built sometime before the tenth century B.C. To reach
the shaft, the citizens of Jerusalem walked down a stepped tunnel
and through a horizontal tunnel, which took them to the top
of the 52-foot- deep shaft. Standing at the top of the shaft, they
could draw water in buckets from the spring chamber below.*

Inside Hezekiah's Tunnel. Two crews of workmen, .
beginning at opposite ends of this eighth-century B.C.
tunnel, chiseled through the rock until they broke through
to each other. The completed 1,750-foot-long tunnel carried
water from the Gihon Spring outside the city walls of ancient
Jerusalem to a pool safely within the city.

Nahman Avigad's excavations in the Jewish Quarter of the Old City uncovered a piece of an ancient city wall, 7 m (c. 23 ft.) thick, of which he excavated a sector 65 m (213 ft.) long, as well as the remains of a strong tower that had been constructed by either Hezekiah or his son Manasseh. These discoveries have proved that the eastern part of the western hill was included in Jerusalem's walled city at least from Manasseh's time, and perhaps even from the days of King Hezekiah.[77]

The excavations of Kenyon from 1961 to 1963 and of Ute Lux from 1970 to 1971, both carried out to the southeast of the Holy Sepulchre, have revealed that this area lay outside the city of Jerusalem in the first century A.D. and that it was not incorporated

---

[77] Avigad, in Yadin, ed., *Jerusalem Revealed*, p. 43; id., in *IEJ* 27 (1977): 56; id., *Discovering Jerusalem* (Nashville, Tenn., 1983), pp. 23-60.

into the city until the time of Hadrian in the second century A.D.[78] This discovery has not settled the question whether the Holy Sepulchre stands on the authentic site of Christ's crucifixion and burial, but it makes it possible to accept the traditional site as authentic.

Extensive excavations over a large area south and southwest of the Temple area were conducted by Benjamin Mazar from 1968 to 1977. The results of his work are of special significance for a better understanding of New Testament Jerusalem. He found evidence that the southwest entrance of the Temple was not reached via a bridge of many arches that was thought to have connected the western hill of Jerusalem with the Temple hill, but that it was reached by a staircase leading from the bottom of the Tyropoeon Valley via a one-arched bridge up to the Royal Stoa in the outer Temple court. Furthermore, Mazar uncovered the exceedingly impressive monumental stairway, 64 m (c. 210 ft.) wide and consisting of 30 steps, which led from a plaza south of the Temple area to the Double Gate in the southern wall of the Temple platform. This gate gave access to the outer Temple court, the Court of the Gentiles, via a sloping subterranean ramp that reached the surface of the court just north of the Royal Stoa. One has to see these remains of New Testament Jerusalem to appreciate fully the beauty of that city in the time of Jesus.[79]

Mazar's excavations uncovered many rows of masonry in the Temple platform's southern retaining wall built by Herod the Great. In some places, 34 rows of masonry, each 1.14 m (c. 3¾ ft.) thick are preserved, and some of these blocks of stone are 10.5 m (c. 34½ ft.) long. They are beautifully cut and fit so well together that no mortar was needed between the individual blocks of stone. Protected by debris for nearly 2,000 years, the stones of the recently excavated parts of the Herodian wall have not weathered; they look as if they had just left the stone masons' hands.[80] Seeing this wall helps one to

---

[78] Kenyon, *Digging Up Jerusalem*, pp. 226-235, 261; Lux, "Vorläufiger Bericht über die Ausgrabung unter der Erlöserkirche im Muristan in der Altstadt von Jerusalem in den Jahren 1970 and 1971," *Zeitschrift des Deutschen Palästina Vereins* 88 (1972): 184-201.

[79] In Yadin, ed., *Jerusalem Revealed*, pp. 25-35; id., *The Mountain of the Lord* (Garden City, N. Y., 1975).

[80] Mazar, *Jerusalem Revealed*, photo on p. 34.

understand better how Jesus' disciples looked with awe and admiration on Jerusalem's Temple structures (Matthew 24:1). Parts of the paved street have been excavated outside of and along the western and southern retaining walls of the Herodian Temple platform. On this pavement many large blocks of stone lay in a great tumble, just where they had fallen when buildings above the street were destroyed by Titus' soldiers in 70 A.D.

Before leaving this part of our survey I want to emphasize that I have by no means done justice to the wealth of material found in the excavations of the sites mentioned. I have referred to very few objects discovered in the course of these excavations, and have been influenced in the choice of the sites more or less by my own interests.

Robinson's Arch. This artist's reconstruction shows the southern and western area of the Temple Mount as it may have looked in King Herod's Jerusalem (first century A.D.). Benjamin Mazar's Temple Mount excavations from 1968 to 1977 led him to conclude that the southwest entrance to the Second Temple precincts was reached via the stairway supported by the one-arched bridge at the southwest corner of the Temple Mount.

Eighth-century B.C. Israelite city wall in Jerusalem.
The broad wall, here seen with a man standing upon it,
is set amid a tracery of smaller walls and house
foundations of the eighth to seventh century B.C. The
massive wall was uncovered in 1970 by Nahman Avigad
in the Jewish quarter of Jerusalem's Old City. The
discovery of this angled wall was a crucial piece of
evidence for determining the size of Jerusalem in the
eighth century B.C.

*Monumental staircase along the south wall of the
Temple Mount. More than 200 feet across, this broad
staircase led from the southern part of Jerusalem on the
Ophel Hill to a double doorway, now sealed, built into
Herod's Temple enclosure wall. Excavated by Benjamin
Mazar, the stairway has been partially restored.*

Ophel Hill: The stepped structure. At the right of this photo is a 50-foot-high stepped structure erected on the rubble of 13th-century B.C. Canaanite remains. The structure has been dated to the pre-Davidic Jebusite period in Jerusalem; it may have been reused by both David and Solomon in their building projects. While its purpose is not entirely clear, the structure may have been part of the support for an earthen platform that would have stood prominently, high above the city of the time, perhaps supporting an important royal building.

The modest walls and steps in the lower left of the photo belong to a domestic house of the eighth or seventh century B.C. and are typical of Israelite house architecture exposed on this slope.

"To the place of trumpeting to [declare]. . . . " This inscribed stone stood on the pinnacle of the southwest corner of the Temple Mount until it toppled to the pavement below during the destruction of the Temple by the Romans in 70 A.D. The complete inscription probably continued with a reference to the Sabbath; the shofar, or ram's horn, was blown by a priest standing near this inscription, to announce the beginning and the end of the weekly holy day.

Some readers would probably have liked to see included such important excavation sites as Bethel, Ein Gedi, Gezer, Gibeah, Gibeon, Heshbon, Lachish, Megiddo, Taanach, Tirzah, or others. I realize that all these sites and many others have made significant contributions to our understanding of biblical history, culture and religion, but time and space have imposed their limits. The fact that so much material is not being discussed in this survey emphasizes what I said at the outset—that the amount of archaeological evidence unearthed during the last 37 years is so overwhelming that it is impossible to treat it all adequately in a brief survey.

7
NEW TESTAMENT
DISCOVERIES

This section overlaps with the previous one, because evidence from some excavation sites already discussed, such as Qumrân and Jerusalem, shed significant light on New Testament studies. But let me refer to a few important New Testament discoveries that have not yet been mentioned.

A good number of papyri containing New Testament books of the early centuries have either been discovered or published during the last 37 years. Foremost among them are the Bodmer papyri from Egypt, some of which date from as early as the end of the second century. Among these papyri is also the earliest presently existing copy of the two epistles of Peter, dating to the third century.[81]

A survey would be incomplete if no mention were made of the 13 Gnostic codices discovered at Nag Hammadi in 1946, published in 1956 and onward. Some scholars claim that these Coptic documents, totaling about 1,200 manuscript pages, are of greater importance to biblical studies than the Dead Sea Scrolls. I must leave a true evaluation of their significance to my New Testament colleagues.[82]

During the excavations of Caesarea, two extremely important fragmentary stone inscriptions were found, one mentioning Pontius Pilate as prefect of Judea,[83] and the other referring to Nazareth as the

---

[81] Floyd V. Filson, "A New Papyrus Manuscript of the Gospel of John," BA 20 (1957): 54-63; id., "The Bodmer Papyri," BA 22 (1959): 48-51; id., "More Bodmer Papyri," BA 25 (1962): 50-57.

[82] Victor R. Gold, "The Gnostic Library of Chenoboskion," BA 15 (1952): 70-88; Filson, "New Greek and Coptic Gospel Manuscripts," BA 24 (1961): 2-18; A. K. Hembold, The Nag Hammadi Gnostic Texts and the Bible (Grand Rapids, Mich., 1967); James M. Robinson, ed., The Nag Hammadi Library (New York, 1977).

[83] A.Frova, "L'iscrizione di Ponzo Pilato a Cesarea," Rendiconti, Istituto Lombardo, Accademia di Scienze e Lettere, 95 (1961): 419-434; J. Vardaman, "A New Inscription Which Mentions Pilate as 'Prefect,'" JBL 81 (1962): 70-71.

seat of the priestly family of Hapizzez after the Bar Kokhba rebellion.[84] The Pilate inscription was found by A. Frova during his Italian expedition's excavation of the Roman theater of Caesarea in 1961. It

Pontius Pilate inscription. This temple dedicatory stone was found reused as a theater step in Caesarea. The Latin text reads: "Pontius Pilate, the Prefect of Judea, has dedicated to the people of Caesarea a temple in honor of Tiberius."

[84] Avi-Yonah, " A List of Priestly Courses from Caesarea," *IEJ* 12 (1962): 136-139.

is of great importance, because it is the first attestation, outside of the testimony of the Bible and of Josephus, of the governorship of Pilate over Palestine from the first century A.D.

The Nazareth inscription, found during Michael Avi-Yonah's excavation of Caesarea in 1962, is of even greater significance, because Nazareth is nowhere mentioned in ancient sources outside of the New Testament. Its name does not occur in the Old Testament, nor in Josephus, nor in the Jewish non-biblical literature. For this reason, some critical scholars had even questioned its existence in New Testament times. The discovery of this inscription was therefore an extremely significant event.

In 1968, the first remains of a victim of a crucifixion were excavated. A rock-cut Jewish tomb in the Jerusalem suburb of Giv'at ha-Mivtar was accidentally opened by a construction crew. The skeleton was found in a stone burial box called an ossuary. Both heel bones had been pierced by a large iron nail, and the shinbones had been broken intentionally. The man, whose name Yehohanan was incised on his coffin, was between 24 and 28 years old when he was executed. Osteological study showed that the young man was 1.68 m (5 ft. 6 in.) tall and had evidently never been engaged in heavy work during his life. He may have belonged to a wealthy family. He may have been a scholar or teacher who was executed for a political crime. The archaeological evidence shows that his crucifixion took place in the first century A.D. before the fall of Jerusalem in 70 A.D., hence during the time of Jesus' ministry or soon thereafter. The position of the heel bones pinned together by a long iron nail show that Yehohanan had been crucified in an unnatural and extremely painful position. His exact position on the cross has been the subject of different interpretations among scholars.[85] This discovery gives us a rather clear picture of the sufferings and humiliation Jesus endured.

In the summer of 1978, I visited St. Catherine's Monastery at the foot of Mt. Sinai for the fifth time. An Israeli guide told me of a sensational discovery that I had already heard something about in a

---

[85] Vassilios Tzaferis, "Jewish Tombs at and Near Giv'at ha-Mivtar, Jerusalem," *IEJ* 20 (1970): 18-32; id., "Crucifixion—The Archaeological Evidence," *BAR* XI:1 (Jan./Feb. 1985): 44-53; N. Haas, "Anthropological Observations on the Skeletal Remains from Giv'at ha-Mivtar," *IEJ* 20 (1970): 49-59; Yadin, "Epigraphy and Crucifixion," *IEJ* 23 (1973): 18-22; V. Moller-Christensen, "Skeletal Remains from Giv'at ha-Mivtar," *IEJ* 26 (1976): 35-38.

Mosaic of Jesus. Using dentist's tools, a restorer carefully scrapes away centuries of dirt to reveal a brilliantly colored, full-figure mosaic of Jesus. Jesus is the focal point in the mosaic of the Transfiguration at St. Catherine's Monastery at the foot of Mt. Sinai. Created at the command of Emperor Justinian the Great (527-565), the mosaic covers the apse of the church.

vaguely worded newspaper report. Since then several brief announcements have appeared in *Biblical Archaeologist* and elsewhere.[86] Pieced together, the various bits of information indicate that in 1975 a fire broke out in one of the structures built against the inside of the monastery wall and caused some damage. In the course of the subsequent repairs, workmen accidentally broke into an unknown small room and found several boxes containing manuscripts. Since that discovery, three Greek scholars from Athens have been allowed to study and microfilm the material in the monastery, but they have not yet released an official report of their work and findings. According to secondhand reports, the discovered material consists of patristic and liturgical texts on parchment and papyrus, which originated between the fourth and ninth centuries. The most startling item in these reports is that there are among the manuscripts some additional pages of the incomplete, fourth-century Bible that Constantin von Tischendorf discovered in the same monastery more than a hundred years ago. I refer to the famous Codex Sinaiticus, which is now one of the priceless treasures in the British Museum in London.

---

[86] S. Agrourides and J. H. Charlesworth, "A New Discovery of Old Manuscripts on Mt. Sinai: A Preliminary Report," *BA* 41 (1978): 29-31; Charlesworth, " St. Catherine's Monastery: Myths and Mysteries," *BA* 42 (1979): 174-179; id., *The Manuscripts of St. Catherine's Monastery: A Preliminary Report on the Manuscripts* (Winona Lake, Ind., 1981).

8
CONCLUSION

Looking back on the exciting discoveries made in biblical archaeology during the last three and one half decades, one cannot help but feel as did Ulrich von Hutten, a humanist who lived during the Renaissance and the Reformation. Von Hutten said that he frequently thanked God for allowing him to live in a time when it was so interesting and inspiring to be alive. During the last few decades, as discoveries that illuminate the Bible in so many aspects have been made, I also have often been excited and grateful to see such a bright light shining on the Bible in my time.

Those who believe that the text of the Bible came into our hands essentially unaltered have had their belief strengthened by the discoveries of scores of biblical Hebrew manuscripts. It has warmed my heart to see that discoveries made in the Bible lands have provided evidence that an alphabetic script existed in the time of the earliest Bible writers, and that many historical details of the Old and New Testament stories are historically reliable. And the exciting finds that are constantly being made in the ancient lands of the Bible are catching the imagination of many earnest students of the Bible, as is clearly proved by the increasing popularity of periodicals or books dealing with biblical archaeology. Who knows what the next decades will reveal? No one can predict what the soil of Israel or Mesopotamia will bring to light before another 37 years roll by. However, if the last 37 years are an indication of what can be expected, then we cannot set our hopes too high.

ABBREVIATIONS